HONOUR BEAT

Honour Beat

Tara Beagan

Honour Beat
first published 2019 by Scirocco Drama
An imprint of J. Gordon Shillingford Publishing Inc.

Scirocco Drama Editor: Glenda MacFarlane

Cover artwork by Andy Moro, from a photo of Monique Mojica
Cover design by Doowah Design

Author photo by Tara Beagan
Production photos by Brian Harder

Printed and bound in Canada on 100% post-consumer recycled paper.
We acknowledge the financial support of the Manitoba Arts Council and The Canada Council for the Arts for our publishing program.

Production inquiries, please contact the playwright at:
tb@article11.ca

Library and Archives Canada Cataloguing in Publication

Title: Honour beat / Tara Beagan.

Names: Beagan, Tara, author.

Description: First edition. | A play.

Identifiers: Canadiana 20190056789 | ISBN 9781927922477 (softcover)

Classification: LCC PS8603.E34 H66 2019 | DDC C812/.6—dc23

J. Gordon Shillingford Publishing
P.O. Box 86, RPO Corydon Avenue, Winnipeg, MB Canada R3M 3S3

dedicated to every Indigenous woman who cut the path,
that we could make the space to walk together

Tara Beagan

Born in Niitsitapi country, Tara Beagan is a proud Ntlaka'pamux and Irish "Canadian" halfbreed. She has written more than twenty plays, and also directs and performs. Currently, she co-helms ARTICLE 11 with her most cherished collaborator, favourite artist, and true love, Andy Moro. A11, now based in Mohkintsis, has brought Indigenous activist artworks to the NAC, the ROM, Kingcome Inlet, Kamloops, Winnipeg, Saskatoon, Calgary's City Hall, the Edinburgh Fringe, Gadigal Country (Sydney Festival), and Wellington, Aotearoa (NZ).

Playwright's Note

This work is a celebration of women. Women Elders and mentors have guided me throughout my life, and continue to do so. Late Great Aunties Diane and Hazel, dear cousins Sharon and Cathy, innumerable Aunties of the heart, cherished theatre and literary mentors, my older sister Rebecca, her daughter Diana, and of course – my Mom, Pauline.

We are the ones who carry. Whether we become mothers or not, we share the gift of carrying our children to adulthood. We honour those who birthed the children, and come together to share the responsibility of taking care of the young ones as best we can. Of course, other genders help support this undertaking, and I give thanks to them as well. With this play, however, I gently invite everyone to honour those in your own lives who carry. The women.

Women in my circle have given me strength, held me up, illuminated my Creator-given gifts, and returned me to myself when I have become lost. My little life is symbolic of how women have carried our nations into this time. When our Indigenous languages and arts were outlawed, women whispered words and song to babies, keeping those blessings alive. Big sisters passed teachings along to the little sisters, and on we forged.

The deluge of colonization has made sure there are fewer of us than there once were. Those of us who remain and thrive must teach as we are learning, just as Anna-Rae and Rae-Anna must do for one another. Just as Mom does for her "girls." Balancing this trio is an Indigenous man capable of nurturing selflessness, our Spanish. He is rare, but he exists.

When we work together we are more powerful, beautiful, and complete. Veteran Indigenous theatre artists inspired this work – women, all. Your names are woven into this story, I hope you recognize yourselves and my gratitude. With this play I give thanks for every path cut, every stumble along the way, and every story shared.

Foreword

by Senator Lillian Eva Quan Dyck

I was intrigued by Tara Beagan's request to write the foreword to her play; she said that it was inspired by the debate in the Senate on a bill about medical assistance in dying. That particular bill was one that affects everyone, and it was the first time that I felt the Senate was truly nonpartisan in our debates. Senators from all groups spoke from their hearts and I felt we listened respectfully to each other, even though our views were dramatically different. So I read *Honour Beat* with the bill in mind, thinking it would be about the key issue that the Senate identified – the lack of clarity on who could have access to medical assistance in dying. Our main focus in the Senate was on trying to define a grievous and irremediable medical condition in which death was reasonably foreseeable. So I expected that *Honour Beat* might be centred on a person who was trying to convince the medical experts that s/he fit the criteria for a medically assisted death. I was wrong and in fact, the way in which "Mom" arranges her medically assisted death in the play is beautiful. She finds a way to honour her Indigenous roots which transcends the medical and legal technicalities.

The main theme of the play which resonated for me was that of self-identity. All of the characters are of mixed ethnic identity, but the play reveals a whole new, to me, facet about self-identity. As Mom nears death, her daughters are sorting through the family history, trying to make sense of what they know of the paternal line. A surprising twist emerges related to the rape of their grandmother by a priest in an Indian residential school. The play reveals a different story about why girls would attempt to run away from residential school and why they might have died from undocumented causes. I am reminded of the well-known tragic story of Charlie Wenjack. But the story here has a female-specific perspective. We are given a new reason for the deaths and attempts to run away from Indian residential schools.

The play elicits many questions about Indian residential schools: What happened to the girls raped by the priests? What happened to them if they became pregnant? And what happened to their babies? How do the babies who survived and their descendants reconcile their mixed heritage under such circumstances?

Honor Beat makes us think about reconciliation in a very personal way. Brava to the playwright.

Senator Lillian Eva Quan Dyck
January 25, 2019

Production History

Honour Beat premiered at Theatre Calgary in Calgary, Alberta, on September 4, 2018, with the following cast and crew. Programmed by Stafford Arima in his debut season at Theatre Calgary.

MOM ....Paula-Jean Prudat
ANNA-RAE...................Monique Mojica
RAE-ANNA....................Tracey Nepinak
SPANISH......................Bernard Starlight

"Girls" in the video:
Imajyn Cardinal as CEILIDH and Indica Cardinal as KEIRA

Directed by Michelle Thrush

Set & Projection Design by Andy Moro

Costume Design by Jeff Chief

Lighting Design by Patrick Beagan

Stage Manager – Ruby Dawn Eustaquio

Assistant Stage Manager – Sang-Sang Lee

Original Music and Vocals – Pura Fé

Sound Design by Deanna H. Choi

Dramaturg – Jenna Turk

Vocal Coach – Jane MacFarlane

Elder-in-Residence – Marion Lerat

TC Design Intern – Imajyn Cardinal

Bernard Starlight, Monique Mojica, PJ Prudat, and Tracey Nepinak in the Theatre Calgary production of *Honour Beat*. Set and Video by Andy Moro. Lighting by Patrick Beagan. Costumes by Jeff Chief. Photo by Brian Hardy.

PJ Prudat, Monique Mojica, and Tracey Nepinak in the Theatre Calgary production of *Honour Beat*. Set and Video by Andy Moro. Lighting by Patrick Beagan. Costumes by Jeff Chief. Photo by Brian Hardy.

PJ Prudat, Monique Mojica, and Tracey Nepinak in the Theatre Calgary production of *Honour Beat*. Set and Video by Andy Moro. Lighting by Patrick Beagan. Costumes by Jeff Chief. Photo by Brian Hardy.

Monique Mojica and PJ Prudat in the Theatre Calgary production of *Honour Beat*. Set and Video by Andy Moro. Lighting by Patrick Beagan. Costumes by Jeff Chief. Photo by Brian Hardy.

Characters

MOM is around 80, warm and loving. A survivor. She is of unknown Indigenous descent. She is played by a younger woman – a woman who reflects Mom when she felt her strongest and happiest, perhaps in her 30s.

RAE-ANNA is 58, well-organized, a proud wife and mother of two. She is of unknown Indigenous and Euro-Canadian descent. The younger sister.

ANNA-RAE is 62, spiritual, adventurous, and untethered. Of unknown Indigenous descent, though partly of the West Coast. The older sister.

SPANISH is 35 to 45, a mixie of unknown Indigenous and Euro-Canadian descent. Kind and intelligent, he is a care worker and licensed practical nurse.

A palliative hospital room in Toronto, 2018.

Four in the morning.

RAE sits beside the bed which holds her MOM. MOM is dressed in a ruffly pinkish nightgown. RAE finds a video on her phone, then watches it – she and her mother (as her actual age) a mere six months ago.

<u>VIDEO:</u>

MOM: Are you taking a picture right now?

RAE: No.

MOM: Oh. Okay. That would be weird.

They laugh a little.

RAE: No kidding!

MOM: So anyways… I found –

RAE stops the video.

RAE: Aw, Mom. Can you hear me? *(Beat.)* Oh! Here…

RAE finds another video – two young Indigenous females singing a Travelling Song. She holds it close to MOM, in view for her.

It's the girls.

RAE is working hard to sing along, though very softly. When she hears someone approach she abruptly stops the video.

ANNA enters, a flurry of essential oils, accessories and colour. RAE checks the time on her phone.

RAE: Sound the trumpets.

ANNA: Mom! I'm here. I'm sorry I took so long.

ANNA kisses her MOM.

RAE: So, they don't have cell service in South Dakota?

ANNA: Little sister.

ANNA and RAE hug rather without warmth.

RAE: It's been a long time.

ANNA: Just over a year.

RAE: We invite you every Christmas.

ANNA: It's always a busy time at the studio. New resolutions, new interest in yoga.

RAE, seeing her sister's shoulders.

RAE: You're all scabby!

ANNA: I was at ceremony, Rae.

ANNA takes a small cloth bundle of medicine from her purse and sets it on the bedside table.

This is from the sundance grounds, Mom. I was told I should bring it to you. I wish you coulda come.

RAE: What is that?

ANNA: Do you really want to know?

RAE: No.

ANNA: Well then, it's from South Dakota. Period.

RAE: Um-hm.

ANNA: Did you put her in this?

RAE: Four in the morning! You could have called once you knew you were on your way.

ANNA: I texted. She hates pink.

RAE: It's not pink, it's mauve – What took you so long?

ANNA: Do you really want to know, or are you just pissy because I didn't ask "How high?" when you said "Jump"?

RAE: First you neglect to tell me you're leaving the country. Then I call you a dozen times and text you another – No. Never mind.

ANNA: I texted I was catching the first flight out! That flight was three hours away from when I got your messages, and there is precious little I could do about that!

RAE: The Lakota Sioux don't have any travel gods who coulda sped that up?

ANNA takes a deep breath.

Beat.

She needs constant care.

ANNA: A roster of five first-rate home care workers – workers she hand-picked! – rotating on eight-hour shifts around the clock.

RAE: Just – You should have told me.

ANNA: Fine.

Beat.

A loud, intrusive hospital sound blasts into their space.

Is it just me, or is this hospital extra shitty?

RAE: It's pretty bad. But. She was only in Emergency for an hour. By some miracle. Then this bed became available.

ANNA: I suppose she was strapped into a stretcher, on display in a chaotic hallway.

RAE: She wouldn't wake up, Anna. And she was alone. So I told the worker to call an ambulance.

ANNA: She wanted to spend her final moments at home. You know that.

RAE: This city is not "home" for Mom. She just lives here.

ANNA: For crying out loud.

RAE: Well, you're the one who hauled her four thousand kilometres away from the city she's spent over sixty years –

ANNA: Some people consider this a viable city to live in, Rae-Anna. Like, about three million people.

RAE: Those same people elected Rob Ford.

ANNA: Literally anywhere is better than an old folks' home in Surrey.

RAE: It's a beautiful facility! And it was close enough to us that we could have visited every week. Several times a week, time permitting. Her friends, too.

ANNA: Ya, well, she made her choice.

RAE: And who talked her into moving here?

ANNA: She has friends here, Rae. She's created community. There's all kinds of Indians here. It's the fucking gathering place.

RAE: Is that from the brochure?

ANNA: You know she'd be saying "Sting Rae" right about now.

RAE: She hasn't called me that in years.

ANNA: Not to your face.

RAE: Did you just come here to argue with me?

ANNA: I live here. You are the visitor.

RAE: Because you stole our mother away from her rightful hometown –

ANNA: I have the studio! I make a good living. I couldn't uproot my whole practice, my life, my staff's lives –

RAE: You had no problem doing that to Mom.

ANNA: – and continue to earn enough to support her. Pay for home care. Homeopathic treatments.

RAE: We help with all that.

ANNA: I know you do.

RAE: Yet here she is dying in a hospital room –

ANNA: YOU CALLED THE AMBULANCE THAT BROUGHT HER HERE.

RAE: I didn't. The home care worker did.

Beat.

When I… asked her to.

ANNA turns from RAE.

ANNA: Mom? You're doing so good. You look like one of those toilet paper dolls from the seventies, but we can fix that. You're gonna be home in no time.

RAE: Why would you say that?

ANNA: That's how we say it.

RAE: What?

ANNA: You should know.

ANNA takes out her phone and takes a photo of her MOM in the bed.

RAE: What are you doing?

ANNA: It's for her Facebook group. "Maverick/Matriarchs."

RAE: Matriarchs. Yes. I've been meaning to talk to you about that.

ANNA puts a pink slipper on her own head and takes a selfie with MOM.

ANNA: She'll want them to know where she's at.

RAE: Stop.

ANNA: They're her social lifeline.

RAE: Stop that!

ANNA: You need to calm the hell down. You don't think she can hear you? How about feel you, huh? Do you believe other people have feelings?

RAE: I don't want to fight with you, Anna.

ANNA: Prove it.

RAE: You owe me an apology. For not letting me know you were going on holiday.

ANNA: Holiday? Do you seriously think going to sundance is a holiday?

RAE and ANNA speak the following lines simultaneously:

RAE: I don't care to know. ANNA: It's ceremony, Rae!

RAE: You should have told me you were abandoning her!

ANNA: I'm not new to this. She's been living with me for a year.

Beat.

Why don't you just admit what you're really angry about?

Beat.

You know she hates hospitals. You know she has a DNR order.

RAE: She doesn't need resuscitation! She just won't wake up.

ANNA points to the IV stand.

ANNA: What is this?

RAE: It's just saline.

ANNA: That sounds delicious.

RAE shoots a "What?" look at her sister.

I haven't eaten. Or had water. For a couple days.

RAE: They have water on the plane.

ANNA: I don't drink that Monsanto crap. And I would love to wash up.

RAE: I can't imagine why you'd put yourself through that.

ANNA: It is ceremony.

RAE: We're not even Sioux.

ANNA: You did a little research.

RAE: A quick Google. No big whoop. God knows what you were off doing. I had to know whether to expect you to survive or not. Not that the gory details inspired any faith around that.

ANNA: When exactly did she lose consciousness?

RAE: We don't know exactly. The last two workers on shift noted she seemed very tired. Thought maybe she just needed a good rest. But when the girl went in to wake her up this morning, she wouldn't.

ANNA: What time was that?

RAE: Nine a.m. here. Six in Vancouver.

RAE hands ANNA a notebook, their MOM's care workers' journal. ANNA looks inside.

I panicked, Anna. Some stranger tells me my Mom won't wake up. I'm four thousand kilometres away…

ANNA: She's not a stranger.

RAE: She's not you!

Beat.

ANNA: I'm sorry I wasn't here, Mom.

RAE: You can't be at someone's side all the time.

ANNA, overwhelmed, processes this kindness.

ANNA: I… I should have told you I was going.

Now RAE is overwhelmed.

Where is the washroom?

RAE: Back there. (*Beat.*) But I think it's just for patients, though.

ANNA heads back behind the curtain.

Public uses the one down the hall, past the elevators.

We hear the door close behind the curtain.

(*Sighs.*) Why do I bother?

RAE's phone is vibrating.

She puts her earbuds in and takes a FaceTime call.

We see but don't hear CEILIDH, in her room. CEILIDH's responses are in parentheses.

Hi, Ceilidh, honey. Are you ok? (*Ya. But. Auntie said you're upset.*) Oh, she did? (*She got there?*) Ya, she finally – hunny. The wifi is pretty crappy here, so – *(SHE GOT THERE?)* Yes, she got here. But you might – reception is – Hey, I told you to get some sleep. It's one in the morning for you! *(Put her on!)* She's in the bathroom. Texting you, I guess. When she comes out I'm going to try to get her to agree to bring your Gram back to Vancouver, okay? *(She won't like that.)* No, I know she won't. *(Don't bully her.)* I won't. I don't do that! *(Hm.)* You sound more like your auntie every day. *(The signal makes CEILIDH pixelate and freeze, choppy.*) Ceilidh? Hun? Hello?

SPANISH enters, wearing scrubs. He carries a tray with three travel coffee cups and a soup. He knocks lightly and then comes in.

SPANISH: Hello? (*He sees RAE is on FaceTime. He waves and mouths –*) Hey.

RAE only glares at him.

RAE: Okay, Ceilidh?

CEILIDH's picture returns.

I gotta go, honey. There's a… *(Did you put Grams in a crazy dress or nightie?)* What? *(Ruffly and pink?)* Who… where'd you hear that? *(Online. The Mavericks.)* Oh, her Facebook group. Um. Well… No. It's mauve. Try to get some sleep. Your auntie can manage without you. She's a grown woman. *(Be nice to her.)* I am nice! You never mind, you sassy frass. *(Love you, Mom.)* Okay. Love you, too. Buh bye.

SPANISH: Hey. Sorry to interrupt. I'm – hi. You must be Rae-Anna. (*He looks at the coffee cups and hands her one.*) I have the order. This is yours. This is for Anna-Rae. And the broth. For when she's ready.

RAE: Thank you.

SPANISH: I'm Spanish. I'm a friend of your Mom's. And Anna's. (*To MOM.*) Heya, Battleaxe. Lookin' sharp.

RAE looks at him, indignant.

It's a joke. We have. Together. She calls me Cotton Puff. Because of… you know… when you draw blood or… um. And I call her Battleaxe. (*He looks back at the coffees.*) Hey! This one's mine. Ha. (*Beat.*) Okay. Cool. Um. I'll just, uh… go back out. Until Anna's back. If you can let her know… (*Beat.*) Cool.

SPANISH leaves.

RAE takes the lid off her coffee. Looks like her drink. She looks off, the way SPANISH came and went. She sniffs the drink. Sips it. Replaces the lid.

ANNA returns.

ANNA: The asswipe is like sandpaper. Just like the health care system, I guess. "Hey, arseholes – we know this is painful, but we're your only choice."

RAE: She can hear you!

ANNA: Very good, Rae-Anna.

RAE: I see you posted the pictures you took.

ANNA: I told you I was.

RAE: Mm-hm. Well, the girls have seen them and it's made them worried, so… thanks for that.

ANNA: Don't they know what's going on here?

RAE: Somewhat.

ANNA: Okay.

RAE: You don't have kids, Anna-R –

ANNA: Some of us choose not to have kids, Rae-Anna.

RAE: Don't we all know it!

ANNA: Creator willing.

ANNA sees her tea and takes it up.

Oh! Saving grace.

RAE: Someone delivered these.

ANNA shakes her head.

What?

ANNA: You seriously think the hospital provides fair trade coffee? *(Noticing the broth.)* And *(Picking up the thermos.)* is this for me?

RAE: Yes. He says it's broth. How – ?

ANNA: That was Spanish. Didn't he introduce himself?

RAE: Kinda.

ANNA: He's a friend.

RAE: Ah.

ANNA: What?

RAE looks away, shrugging. She sips her coffee.

Well, go ahead. If you're gonna.

RAE looks at her phone.

RAE: I didn't say a thing.

ANNA: He's a nurse.

RAE does some typing on her phone.

RAE: Good for him.

ANNA: He's putting himself through medical school.

RAE: I'm sure he's an excellent student.

ANNA: He's a licensed nurse practitioner right now, but he –

RAE: Anna. I didn't ask. And not to be rude, but I don't care. I can't keep track, so I've stopped trying.

ANNA breathes deeply.

And don't roll your eyes at me.

ANNA: I am merely breathing.

RAE: Yes, well. I need to go outside for some fresh air and make some calls. Are you staying?

ANNA: I'm not coming outside to watch you smoke, if that's what you're asking. I thought you quit.

RAE: I'm asking if you're staying with Mom while I get some air and check my voicemail. I don't want her left alone.

ANNA: I'm here.

RAE: I asked them to test her vitals. They should be coming in with the machine thingy soon – I hope – so I'm just making sure you're gonna be here.

ANNA: THANK YOU, RAE. FOR CALLING ME AT CEREMONY AND MAKING SURE I WOULD BE HERE.

Beat. The sisters face off.

She said I should go.

Beat.

She asked me to dance for us. Pray. For us. For me and you.

RAE doesn't know how to answer.

RAE: Well. We're here now.

ANNA: We're here now.

RAE leaves.

ANNA takes a moment to breathe and connect. She takes MOM's hand.

ANNA softly sings the Travelling Song. This wakes MOM, but only to her. Medically, MOM is still unconscious.

MOM: You know she means well.

ANNA: I do. But does *she*?

MOM: Anna.

ANNA: I know… be patient.

MOM: Yes.

ANNA: You've told me that a thousand times. And always so patiently.

MOM: (*Laughs, then notices her nightgown.*) Oh. This is awful.

ANNA: Don't worry. Rae assured me it is not pink.

MOM: (*She remembers.*) Oh, right. I had it on my list.

ANNA: What list?

MOM: The one for Spanish. For once I conked out. What he should do.

ANNA: Of all things, you asked for this nightgown? What are you doing penance for?

MOM: Your sister has graciously never pointed out that I don't wear the clothes she gifts me. And so… I didn't want her to find my Rae bin.

ANNA: …?

MOM: All the presents she's given me over the years. Things I used to put out when she was over. Knick-knacks and little candy dishes and that. The clothes, though… I meant to donate them somewhere but I never had the heart.

ANNA: Well. What can we expect from a woman who goes to a McChurch in a strip mall?

MOM: She buys for others the things she'd love to receive herself. It's well intended.

ANNA: No reason you should be drowned in doilies.

MOM: You can spare your own sister some of the forgiveness you grant others, my girl.

ANNA: I know. I do. And I'm trying.

MOM: I asked Spanish to dress me in something from my Rae bin when she was on her way.

ANNA: You have a list of requests that only Spanish knows?

MOM: You're a hell of a warrior. But you can't do everything, my girl.

MOM holds her arms out to hug ANNA. They hug.

The next sequences happen concurrently, one outdoors, one inside the hospital room. During the course of the play, this will happen several times.

OUTDOOR SCENE:

RAE arrives outside. Dark, quiet night.

She opens her phone and finds the video of the girls singing.

She puts her earbuds in and listens.

<u>*VIDEO*</u>

> *We see the girls floating around their MOM, auntie and grams.*

RAE's emotions bring her to a seated position.

She listens a little while longer, then stops the video.

She holds the phone to her heart, breathing.

She pockets the phone and glances around, checking for people. Nobody is around.

She finds a hidden joint and lights it up. Deep hauls.

She finds a song she loves on her phone and listens to it, grooving while she inhales deeply.

This relaxes her.

In The Hospital Room:

MOM and ANNA are holding each other gently.

ANNA: What happened?

MOM: I got old.

ANNA: But I was only gone three days!

MOM: Life passes in a blink. I'm not a day over thirty-five! Until a few days ago. Now I'm thirty-five and eighty-one.

ANNA: That's a hundred-and-twenty…something.

MOM: No wonder!

ANNA: Have you been in pain?

MOM: No. I wouldn't have kept it from you.

ANNA: No?

MOM: Okay, I would have tried. But I wasn't.

ANNA: You shoulda went in for surgery, Mom. A twenty percent chance is still twenty percent.

MOM: Your sister said the same thing.

ANNA: Well, I hate to agree, but –

MOM: No. No more. There's been enough poking and prodding at this ole sack of bones. Nineteen – tonsillectomy. Forty-five – hysterectomy. Fifty-five – mastectomy. Sixty-one – knee replacement. Seventy-one – second mastectomy. Enough. What is my hair doing?

ANNA: I'll fix it.

ANNA takes MOM's hair down and starts to braid it.

MOM: How was sundance?

ANNA: So incredible, Mom. The sunsets in South Dakota are… the sky dancing with the land. I danced for you. And for Rae. Me and Rae.

MOM: And now we're all together. First time since I left Vancouver.

ANNA: Smarty-pants.

MOM: Takes one to know one.

ANNA: She's lashing out.

MOM: She's afraid.

ANNA: So am I.

MOM: Not the way she is. She's afraid she isn't able to do enough. You know you're doing what you can.

ANNA: She subscribes to a fear-based religion.

MOM: Well. No point talking about that today. Any likes on our picture?

ANNA: Twenty-six, last time I checked. And that was within minutes of posting.

MOM: Yes!

ANNA: I don't want you in this place, Mom. We worked so hard to keep you out of that home. Being here just feels wrong.

MOM: Tell me about it.

ANNA: Beeping and sweeping and cold hands handling you. Dousing themselves in sanitizer before and afterwards.

MOM: I didn't mean really tell me about it. I'm in it, I don't need a paint by number.

OUTDOOR SCENE, Continued:

SPANISH arrives outside. SPANISH puts his ID badge in the door to prop it open.

SPANISH: Hi Rae. (*Beat.*)

ANNA: Did we do the right thing, Mom? Moving you out here with me?

SPANISH: Or. Sorry. Rae-Anna.

MOM: We've had fun!

ANNA: Ya!

MOM: And I couldn't have survived one day in that evangelical funny farm.

SPANISH: I don't mean to disturb your alone time.

ANNA: Ah, Rae. She's such a weirdo.

SPANISH: I've just… I feel like I should clarify.

MOM: She couldn't take me in.

SPANISH: Can I? Is it okay if we talk for a sec?

RAE does a little dance move that SPANISH takes to mean "Go on."

SPANISH: Oh. 'Kay. Thanks.

MOM: She has her hands full with the girls. And that man she married.

ANNA: I know, but – a Christian Seniors' Home? Barf.

SPANISH: I wanted to let you know that I'm one of your Mom's most trusted care workers.

MOM: She suggested the home she would've chosen for herself.

SPANISH: And that's not a humble brag, that's something I'm truly proud of.

ANNA: She didn't imagine you'd move over four thousand klicks away.

SPANISH: We met about a year ago when she moved out here.

MOM: No. I don't think she saw that coming at all.

SPANISH: Saw each other a fair bit because I work at her oncologist's. And anyway… we kinda hit it off. Me and Anna-Rae too, but…

ANNA: She's an asshole.

SPANISH: Uh… ya.

MOM: She can be.

SPANISH: I'm sure we all agree that what's important now is what's best for your Mom.

ANNA: And she doesn't understand. Refuses to. And she insists on hanging on to her resentment and anger.

SPANISH: Mind if I sit?

RAE moves in such a way that SPANISH takes to mean "No, thank you."

MOM: Hm. You sound kinda mad.

SPANISH: I respect that.

ANNA: And resentful.

MOM: My girl.

SPANISH: Um. I just wanted you to know that I'm a professional. Your Mom's care comes first. Whatever my feelings about Anna.

MOM: Home is where my girls are.

SPANISH: I respect what the circumstances are.

MOM: You may as well learn to love everything about your sister. She's never gonna change.

SPANISH: Anyway. I thought you should know.

ANNA: Neither am I.

MOM: I know. And I love you for it.

Both my girls /
are strong minded, self-actualized women and I'm proud as hell.

ANNA: *(Finishing MOM's sentence along with her.)*
– are strong minded, self-actualized women and I'm proud as hell.

SPANISH: What matters is your mom asked me to – Oh.

RAE is grooving, eyes closed, and SPANISH now sees she is smoking a spliff, not able to hear him, and having her own little time.

ANNA: Can I get you anything?

MOM: How 'bout that song we learned last month at the centre?

SPANISH: Oh. Wow. You haven't… heard a word I've said. (*Smelling the pot smoke.*) Thought maybe a skunk was skunking around… Hoo! Okay. Rewind.

He leaves, replacing his ID badge with a roll of medical tape he fishes out of his pocket. RAE grooves.

ANNA: Song…

ANNA finds something to drum on and sings softly, a bright and soothing song.

As the song concludes, SPANISH enters tentatively, with a vital stats machine.

SPANISH: I should hang around outside the door more often.

ANNA holds a welcoming hand out to him. SPANISH takes it.

He puts his arms around her and she lets him hold her a moment.

MOM lies back down comfortably. SPANISH does not hear her.

MOM: Ah. I wondered if my oldest gal would finally give in.

ANNA: She hasn't given in.

SPANISH: Of course not! That's why she hired a hit man.

They all laugh gently. ANNA shifts away from SPANISH.

She's as stubborn as her daughters.

ANNA: She started it.

MOM: Ask him how I got this bed so fast.

ANNA: Spanish.

SPANISH: Yes?

ANNA: Hector.

SPANISH: Yes, Anna-Rae?

ANNA: You pulled strings.

SPANISH: Ummmm. How so?

ANNA: For this bed. Room.

MOM: He did! Look at his face!

SPANISH: Well. The Royal York was all booked up.

ANNA: Hm.

MOM: I knew it.

SPANISH: Uh. But anyways. Your sister wanted us to check your Mom's levels. (*To MOM.*) I'm gonna steal one of your fingers for a sec, Battleaxe. Oxygen and heart rate tend to be erratic at this point, but I understand the desire for hard stats. Do blood pressure while we're here.

He swipes his ID card and uses a portable stats machine to check MOM's vitals.

The heartbeat sounds swell and stars dance before us.

ANNA: I never learned what those two numbers actually mean.

SPANISH: This one is systolic. It's always higher because it's about the pressure during a heart pump. The lower one, diastolic, is a reading for when the heart is at rest.

MOM: You love it when he talks all fancy.

ANNA: Mom!

MOM: Put it on her, Spanish! Have a listen.

ANNA laughs.

SPANISH: Did you want me to check on you?

ANNA: No thank you.

MOM: I bet your pulse is just guh-GUNG! Guh-GUNG! Ga-GOING!

SPANISH: Your mom's stats have been fairly stable since she got here. They're exactly what they were two hours ago. She knows how to live, this one.

MOM: Good steady drum in here.

ANNA: Do you believe her? About the pain? Not giving warning?

SPANISH: I do. It's unusual but not unheard of. Most people with untreated stage four suffer like hell. But she's been pretty chill. Even these last coupla days.

ANNA: Good.

SPANISH: The best. In some ways. Hard for you, to have no time to adjust, but. I mean… No pain, everything seems to be trucking along and then…

ANNA: We could have eased her home from there.

SPANISH: Sounds like your sister panicked.

MOM: Wicked sense of humour.

ANNA: This is the woman who suggested Mom spend her final days in a fucking Christian seniors' home.

SPANISH: Yeah.

ANNA: Rae's more fucking comfortable in a place like this.

MOM: Anna.

ANNA: Sorry, Mom.

MOM: She was pretty freaked out. Your little sis.

ANNA: The architecture for the earliest hospitals, prisons, and schools in this country all had the same baseline.

SPANISH: Not surprising.

MOM: I taught you that.

ANNA: She taught me that.

SPANISH: She did?

MOM: Residential schools feel exactly like prisons.

ANNA: Yeah.

SPANISH: Well. Residential schools were prisons.

MOM: No wonder we like him so much, hey?

ANNA: And yet Rae…

MOM: Anna.

SPANISH: She is kinda scary. Your sister. She grumbled by me in the hall. She saw me looking, so she chucked her coffee into the garbage. The cup and everything.

ANNA and MOM laugh.

But your Mom noted exactly what drink to get her so… well. Your daughters are mighty as you, Battleaxe. You got one hatchet on each side. *(He does chopping motions and sounds.)* Hi-ya hi-ya!

MOM: My Tomahawk Twins.

ANNA: Rae-Anna is pretty fierce. If only she would use her powers for good.

SPANISH: Her dad was a preacher, right?

ANNA: He thought so.

SPANISH: What does that mean?

ANNA: He was a self-appointed messiah. There was no shortage of them in the 1950s.

SPANISH: That never really stopped, did it?

ANNA: True.

SPANISH: And now we have televised messiahs, podcast messiahs…

ANNA: I still think the storefront messiahs are the creepiest. Preying on people, right in their own neighbourhoods.

SPANISH: So. Rae's dad was an unholy roller.

ANNA: Violent megalomaniac.

SPANISH: And your Dad was…?

ANNA: Just a kid.

SPANISH: Who was at the same residential school as your Mom.

ANNA: Yes. You know this. Why the interrogation?

SPANISH: And your mom's dad was…?

ANNA: You – *(She breathes out the rest of this thought, which is "know this!")* My mom's father was NOT her Dad. He was A Father.

SPANISH: A Catholic priest.

ANNA: Yes.

Beat.

What is your point?

SPANISH: You and Rae know two things about your mom's parents. The guy was a priest and the woman – the girl – was a residential school student.

ANNA: Yeah.

SPANISH: So. A priest, a residential school student – just a kid! – and a preacher. These are the paternal figures in your family.

ANNA: I wouldn't call them that. The only one who did any parenting was Rae's "father" and that was only because he loved having absolute control over us.

SPANISH: And your dad passed when he was still a kid?

Silence.

ANNA: Just turned sixteen. The death certificate says he died five days after he and Mom were supposed to run from the school.

SPANISH: And she went without him.

ANNA: He was supposed to meet her. He didn't show. (*Beat.*) His cause of death is "accidental."

MOM: Nothing they did to us was accidental.

SPANISH: It's a hell of a history you all carry.

Beat.

ANNA: I guess you're taking a psychology course this semester.

SPANISH: (*Beat.*) No.

MOM: Don't you squeeze him out, Anna-conda.

SPANISH: You told me about blood memory. The power of it. How our cells, our spirits… carry our ancestors' stories. The ones you know and those you haven't met. I hold that close.

MOM: My Anna-Rae.

SPANISH: So, I figure… all of your ancestors made you become you. And all of Rae-Anna's made Rae-Anna…

ANNA: Become Rae-Anna.

SPANISH: And the biggest difference is your fathers. So…

ANNA: We're kinda different.

Outside, RAE stands to leave.

SPANISH: And the greatest similarity is…

ANNA: Mom.

MOM: I love you.

RAE exits, re-entering the hospital.

ANNA: Rae will ease up on you eventually. When she knows who you are to Mom.

SPANISH: That's... up to you. Your Mom and I have an agreement. She told you everything. Because she believes you can tell Rae-Anna exactly what she needs to hear. So, no matter how much you flirt with me, I'm sticking to the plan. Her plan.

ANNA smiles a little.

She looks so much softer than I've ever seen her.

MOM: I've seen better days.

ANNA: She's seen better days.

SPANISH: She has lost some weight, hey?

ANNA: Yeah.

SPANISH: Still a mighty presence, though. She's like a mountain wearing a princess costume.

They laugh.

MOM: He ain't wrong.

SPANISH: Is the home-care journal here?

ANNA: Yes! Here.

She hands him the home-care journal.

SPANISH: Hm. Down at sundance... when did you start your fast?

ANNA: The night before last. Thank you for the broth, by the way. And the tea.

SPANISH: Look at this.

He shows her a note in the journal.

ANNA: She didn't eat at all yesterday.

SPANISH: Or drink.

ANNA: Not even water. Mom!

MOM: I wanted to be at ceremony with you.

ANNA: Wanted to know every detail of sundance. I shouldn't have told you.

MOM: I was honoured to learn from you.

SPANISH: Did you find her the moccasins you were hoping for?

MOM: I'm gonna need them.

Finally, ANNA cries. This time, when SPANISH tries to hold her, she takes her own space.

Aw, my girl. Let it out. Crying is good. It clears us out, makes room for the next laugh.

ANNA: Don't be so fucking calm.

SPANISH and MOM speak the following lines simultaneously:

SPANISH: Anna, I'm…

MOM: Calm? I'm not calm, I'm comatose.

ANNA laughs with MOM.

SPANISH: I can leave you alone if you want.

ANNA: I'm not alone.

MOM: I ain't dead yet.

SPANISH: No. Of course. I didn't mean alone-alone. Do you want time alone with your mom? Your sister will be back.

ANNA: Yeah. Just give me a few more minutes, okay?

SPANISH: Okay. You're okay to tell Rae-Anna your Mom's levels?

ANNA: Yeah.

SPANISH: Exact same numbers. Steady drum.

ANNA: Thanks.

MOM: How have you not snapped him up?

SPANISH: I'm right outside the door.

ANNA: Thank you.

They squeeze hands and SPANISH goes, checking his phone as he leaves. ANNA finds the tiny crappy box of tissues the hospital provides. She pulls several of them out – wispy, small, and inadequate.

What are these supposed to do?

MOM: Those couldn't choke a groundhog.

ANNA: I hate it here.

MOM: But you sure like him.

ANNA doesn't answer.

Well?

ANNA: We can't be together.

MOM: But you want to. So does he.

ANNA: It'd be too weird.

MOM: Not at all! He has a gift for caretaking. And he lights up around you.

ANNA: He's pretty cute, alright.

MOM: And loving. That was a beautiful thing he did for his Grannie.

ANNA: Yes. Poor woman.

MOM: But she wasn't alone. She had her devoted grandson.

ANNA: Still a slow, painful death.

MOM: And he guided her home. But didn't get lost, himself. Takes a strong heart.

ANNA: Steady drum.

MOM: Her slow, painful death showed him his gift. She looked after him, even as she journeyed home.

ANNA: Mmm.

MOM: He was lucky he had a Grannie.

ANNA: Yeah.

MOM: Where did he get raised up?

ANNA: Calgary. Alberta.

MOM: Alberta, huh? Cree? No. Blackfoot.

ANNA: All he knows for sure is his white side. His little blonde mama went to Guatemala – on a mission – when she was still in high school. Came back pregnant.

MOM: Hm.

ANNA: What?

MOM: Has he looked into the math on that?

ANNA: What do you mean?

MOM: Well, is he sure his mom didn't go to Guatemala pregnant?

ANNA: I never asked him that.

MOM: I would say he's from closer to home. He'd stick out like a tree on the prairies down there in Guatemala.

ANNA: Ha! All she ever told her parents about the guy was "He's Spanish."

MOM: Ha! He's as Spanish as I am Conservative.

ANNA: So, as soon as he was born, she took off. His grandparents brought him home, nicknamed him "Spanish" and there it stuck.

MOM: She left her baby. Just like that?

ANNA: Well, she was a baby herself.

MOM: So was I.

ANNA: My runaway Mama.

MOM: Wasn't gonna stay at that school.

ANNA: How did you do it, Mom? All by yourself?

MOM: You saved my life, Anna. Gave me hope. Made me feel love. Maybe for the first time.

ANNA: I thought you loved the guy… the kid who knocked you up. My dear ole "Dad."

MOM: Ronnie. We felt we loved each other. But I don't know what happened for sure. I don't know if he tried to meet up with me, or what.

ANNA: But we know he died a few days after you left.

MOM: And so we know it had something to do with him trying to leave.

ANNA: Oh my god, Mom. You don't blame yourself, do you?

MOM: It's possible he was too afraid to leave. That place was the only home he'd ever known.

ANNA: Same for you!

MOM: But I had you inside me. I was making my own home. Becoming one. I'd seen what had happened to some of the other girls who were pregnant. And I couldn't survive that.

ANNA: If his fear was bigger than his love, then you know it wasn't true.

MOM: I was too afraid to stay. What does that say about me?

ANNA: You were born to a student raped by a priest. We don't even know what happened to your little mama. Your fear is deep and it is real.

MOM: I was so afraid.

ANNA: You never had a mom to show you how to live, to love. She was taken from you. You from her.

MOM: I was raised by nuns.

ANNA: You raised yourself.

MOM: The older girls looked after me, really. When they could.

ANNA: Not in the summer.

MOM: Or at Christmas. No. They all had homes to go to. But I only had that school. Me and maybe a dozen or so other kids. Ronnie was one of us.

ANNA: I'm so sorry, Mom.

MOM: No sorries. If I'd had a home to go to, I might never have met my Ronnie. And had you.

ANNA: Mom.

MOM: Imagine! I'd still have the last name some dirty priest stuck me with.

ANNA: So gross.

MOM: Super gross.

ANNA: Change your last name just like that! Just 'cause you wanted to. That's just like you.

MOM: Just like you.

ANNA: You started it!

They laugh.

MOM: Why didn't you ever contact his family?

ANNA: Without you?

MOM: I guess.

ANNA: Mom. I wouldn't go anywhere like that without you.

MOM: I guess it's time you did.

ANNA: Really?

MOM: I think so. Take the girls with you.

ANNA: Okay.

MOM: I'm interested in how a person can forgive someone they never met.

ANNA: Mom…

MOM: I just… tell them I'm sorry.

ANNA: No. No sorries. You didn't do anything wrong.

MOM: I just… sometimes I also feel I might be angry with his family.

ANNA: How are you so beautiful?

MOM: Anyways… you should post that on my Facebook. The forgiving-someone-you-don't-know question. I'd like to know what the other Mavericks think.

ANNA: You're the most forgiving person I know.

MOM: All I do is try to match what I've been given.

ANNA: How so?

MOM: You, Anna. I made lots of mistakes. And you've been so good to me.

ANNA: You're the strongest person I know.

MOM: I wouldn't be if it wasn't for you girls. That's why I need you both here while I journey home.

ANNA: Ah, Mom. I'm sorry.

MOM: It's okay. "We're here now."

ANNA: I just can't understand how she –

MOM: Now's the time, Anna.

ANNA: I know.

MOM: You need to buckle down.

ANNA: How do I… We don't even speak the same language.

RAE returns.

RAE: Did you move her?

ANNA: No.

RAE: She looks different. You moved her.

ANNA: Oh – I fluffed her pillows up a little.

RAE: Why?

ANNA: Ours is not to ask why. Ours is merely to obey.

RAE: Are you telling me she asked you to fluff her pillows?

Beat.

And change her hair?

ANNA shrugs.

Oh, for pete's sake.

ANNA: Who told you to dress her like a cupcake? 'Cause it sure as hell wasn't her!

MOM: Girls…

RAE reaches for the little medicine bundle.

RAE: Can we put this aside for the time being?

ANNA and MOM speak the following lines simultaneously:

ANNA: What? No.

MOM: I like it here.

RAE: You don't see me forcing a Bible into the room.

ANNA: This whole building – country! Is a construct of Christian capitalism.

RAE: Is that boy going to be here the whole time? Waiting for you to summon him for another round of lattes?

ANNA: Spanish is a grown man.

MOM: Yes, he is.

RAE: Mom specifically asked that you and I are the only people –

ANNA: You have the list of her care workers. Home care AND the contacts for Mom's oncologist. Spanish is on that list.

RAE: I assumed it was overflow from your little black book.

ANNA closes her eyes and breathes.

Or your little brown book, I should say. *(She laughs.)* Brown, black, sometimes yellow.

ANNA looks at RAE.

You're like the United Nations of Tinder. *(She giggles some more.)*

MOM and ANNA speak the following lines simultaneously:

MOM: What the heck is Tinder?

ANNA: Tinder?

RAE: *(More giggling.)* Fifty Shades of Shade.

MOM: She's high.

ANNA: You're high.

ANNA smells her sister.

RAE: Don't sniff me! It's undignified.

ANNA: And what is getting stoned at your age?

MOM: Wonderful.

RAE: It's medicinal.

ANNA: For what?

RAE: For Mom.

ANNA: Mom didn't… she doesn't have a prescription for –

RAE: I'm smoking it for her. You judgmental cow.

ANNA: I'm not judging! I'm glad you're admitting to having feeling. Showing some connection to your body. Your emotions.

RAE: You are judging, it's just a different kind of judgment than you usually judge me with.

MOM: Girls.

ANNA: This is why you stopped smoking pot in college. / It makes you paranoid.

RAE: I'm not paranoid. You're judging me.

MOM: Oh, for pete's sake, stop FIGHTING!

Both women look to their MOM.

ANNA suspects RAE heard their MOM.

ANNA: What?

RAE: What?

ANNA: What what?

RAE: Nothing.

Beat.

She didn't eat at all yesterday. Or the day before.

ANNA: That's a problem.

RAE: Yeah.

ANNA takes RAE's hand.

She looks vulnerable. Like a child.

ANNA: We never see her so still.

RAE: And quiet.

MOM: Tsuh!

RAE: And I've no idea when she got so… roly-poly.

MOM: Didn't we just establish that I can hear you?

ANNA: When we were kids, she was so svelte.

RAE: Hourglass. Perfect curves. Tiny waist.

ANNA: Remember she used to say she stayed slim so she could shake the fuzz if they ever caught up to her?

RAE: And then she'd do that little dance.

ANNA: *(Laughs.)* Kinda like disco meets women's traditional.

The sisters do MOM's dance, and MOM joins in. They share that moment of joy.

Beat.

How are the girls?

RAE: Pretty busy. Finals.

ANNA: Right. Seems unfair.

RAE: What?

ANNA: Well, Ceilidh. Offered all those scholarships! Can't they just let her skip finals? What are they gonna do, add bonus points to her perfect grades?

RAE: She's the brains of the family, alright.

ANNA: How do you feel about her choice?

RAE looks at ANNA.

We Skype.

RAE: Right.

ANNA: And text. She said you knew.

RAE: I have no problem with it.

ANNA: Thanks.

RAE: I… I wish she wasn't going so far away, but I'm glad she got her first pick.

ANNA: Selfishly, I'm excited to have her here. And U of T really does have a great law program. A former partner of mine –

RAE: Aboriginal Law. Yes. I hear it's excellent.

Beat.

ANNA: That'll be strange for you. To have her so far away.

RAE: Ya.

MOM: Even more strange for Keira.

ANNA: Even more strange for Keira.

RAE: Ya. They're so close. Or… I should say… Ceilidh is so protective of Keira. Lately they squabble like –

ANNA: Grown-ups?

RAE: Ha.

ANNA: Mom told me she wants what little she has left from the sale of the house to go towards the girls' school. *(Beat.)* I think that's great.

RAE: Thank you.

ANNA: Thank you for looking after all the legal – the money stuff with her.

RAE: We have a good lawyer.

ANNA: And for being executor. Numbers are not my friend.

RAE: Yeah. (*Beat.*) Thank you for... arranging for the ceremonial type stuff. That she wants.

ANNA: I didn't move her out here to take her from you, Rae.

Beat.

I couldn't stand the thought of putting her in a home. Especially that one.

RAE: And I couldn't look after her full-time.

ANNA: I know.

MOM: You're doing beautifully.

RAE: I feel betrayed.

ANNA: By who?

Silence.

RAE: I can't figure that out.

ANNA: Okay.

A moment.

RAE: I keep thinking how awful it will be to pick up her address book and go through each number, dial them, remind myself who I'm calling and then tell them she's gone. And the "I'm so sorry"s and the "My goodness, is there anything I can do?"s.

ANNA: Don't worry. She's outlived most of the people in her address book.

All the women laugh together.

We can take turns.

RAE: Really?

ANNA: Sure.

RAE: And then there's telling all of our friends.

ANNA: Yeah. *(Beat.)* Well, it'll feel like work and then it'll shift. They'll help hold us up.

RAE: Too many fuckin' funerals.

ANNA only looks at RAE.

It's the worst thing about living in Vancouver.

ANNA: Too many fucking funerals.

RAE: And all of them for our women. Men just always seem to get away with it.

ANNA: With what?

RAE: Everything!

ANNA: Yeah.

RAE: Meanwhile women stick around carrying all the weight and burying each other.

MOM: She hears you, Anna-Rae.

Beat.

ANNA: What next?

RAE: Mom said she didn't want the girls to see her like this. Told me it would be "a shameful waste of money to fly those girls out here just to stare at a dying old broad."

ANNA: We went to a memorial gathering a few weeks ago, for our friend Rose, this incredible Anishnaabe woman. Mom was really moved. She was given a lot of teachings that day. *(Beat.)* She asked me to help you and the girls feast their loss of her when they're ready. Feast Mom, really, but that's not how she sees it.

MOM: She won't like it.

RAE: Hm.

MOM: You'll have to help her do it, for the girls' sake.

RAE: Their Dad wouldn't like that.

ANNA: How 'bout you?

Silence.

MOM: Tell her, Anna.

ANNA: I want to look after you.

MOM: Tell her I'm crossing today.

ANNA: Mom…

MOM: Tell her. You know the best way.

ANNA: I need to tell you something.

RAE looks into ANNA's face fully.

Mom… wants me to tell you something.

RAE: 'kay.

ANNA: Spanish… Spanish is here because he's a licensed nurse practitioner.

RAE: Yes, Anna.

ANNA: He –

RAE: Anna. If Mom chose him as one of her care workers, that's great. I don't actually care what you do with him on your own time.

ANNA: This is different, Rae.

RAE: You never hear me. How am I supposed to tell you anything if you never damn well hear me?

ANNA: I'm trying to tell you something.

RAE: I don't care, Anna. I stopped investing in your "relationships" a long time ago. How can I tell you anything if you never hear me?

ANNA: I hear you.

RAE: Oh, God. You know? My whole life... I just want to make you like me. And I see my girls connecting with you, and see how they light up with love from you and I wonder what the hell I ever did to be denied that.

ANNA: We're sisters. I love you no matter what.

RAE: I didn't say "love." I said "like." And I mean "like." You never listen to me, you just hear what you think I'll say.

ANNA: That's not true.

RAE: It is. It always has been. From such a young age, you assumed things about me, and I felt so confused about where those assumptions came from. I couldn't even compete with them. So, I just tried to get them right.

ANNA: I don't know what you're talking about.

RAE: When my Dad left? I was shattered. And you went and told me not to worry about it. That I'd get over it. "That's what Dads do."

MOM: *(To ANNA.)* You didn't.

ANNA: They do.

RAE: So I thought I was supposed to be reacting one way, and tried so hard to do that, when in fact my heart was fucking shattered!

ANNA: Your dad didn't leave, Rae, he fucking died.

RAE: He was driving drunk!

ANNA: It was an accident.

MOM: Not the way he drank.

RAE: Not the way he drank. He was dying that whole time.

MOM: She's right. How many times can we pretend all the harm he did was an accident?

ANNA: Yeah, well. We got used to telling people the bruises and breaks were an accident. They would have taken us from Mom if we hadn't.

RAE: The point is I couldn't even feel him go. You wouldn't let me.

ANNA: I'm sorry, Rae-Anna. I didn't know I had that kind of… influence on you.

Beat. They connect.

RAE: Thank you.

SPANISH enters.

SPANISH: Excuse the interruption. Is this a good time? I can come back.

RAE: If you're doing a muffin run, make mine a doughnut.

Beat.

SPANISH: I can… I can pick some up if that's helpful.

ANNA: He's a nurse, Rae.

RAE: So you say. I'll step outside. You two take your time. But no funny business in front of the matriarch.

SPANISH: Actually, I... wanted to make sure you were updated, Rae-Anna.

ANNA: Shit. Sorry.

RAE: What?

SPANISH: Her vitals. Everything is as it would be. Given her condition. No surprises. We'll want to administer more pain meds in about an hour. If you want to continue with them.

ANNA: What pain meds?

RAE: Through the saline. She hadn't complained of pain, but –

ANNA: Good. Good, Rae. You did good.

SPANISH: Yeah. So. We have to keep an eye on her fluid buildup. Her feet and hands were looking a little puffy. There is a chance her organs just can't process the fluids anymore. Could lead to complications.

RAE: What kind of complications?

ANNA: The kind she wouldn't want treated?

SPANISH: Exactly.

MOM: Maybe just take it out.

SPANISH: Battleaxe. Just gonna check on your hands and feet here.

ANNA: Is the saline against her wishes?

MOM: Yup.

SPANISH: It is.

RAE: I requested it.

MOM: It's okay, Rae-Anna.

ANNA: It's okay, Rae-Anna.

SPANISH: Right now it's helping with comfort.

ANNA: So, should we leave it as is?

MOM: Whatever. Same difference.

SPANISH: I'd advise leaving it and keeping an eye on her.

RAE: Please.

ANNA and MOM speak the following lines simultaneously:

ANNA: Okay.

MOM: Okay.

SPANISH: I'll be here. If anything is needed.

RAE: Well. Thank you, young man.

She awkwardly pats his shoulder.

I need to go step outside. Make a call. If you'll excuse me.

SPANISH: Of course.

She leaves.

ANNA: Weirdo.

SPANISH: You okay?

ANNA: Uh huh. I haven't told her yet.

SPANISH: I'm not pressuring you.

ANNA: I know.

SPANISH: Okay.

MOM: Maybe just a little.

ANNA: How did you know you're the right person for this? I mean, with my mom?

MOM: I knew.

SPANISH: It has to be the right fit. But with your Mom, well… she picked on me so often at the clinic, and I looked forward to it every time, so I figured we'd be good at the serious stuff, too.

ANNA smiles.

And she asked me.

ANNA: She seldom hears "no."

Beat.

SPANISH: I know it's hard, Anna, but I wanted to remind you your Mom stated a preference for sunset or sunrise.

ANNA: That's really soon.

SPANISH: Yeah. And we could keep her around for weeks, maybe, but… it would require some care that she didn't want.

ANNA: I understand.

SPANISH: She mentioned one time how perfect it would be to take her exit just before the new moon, which you'd think… the odds of that are not really in her favour, but…

MOM: Here we are. Tomorrow will be a new day.

ANNA: She's pretty stubborn.

MOM: I love that he remembered that.

SPANISH: She's pretty cool. *(Beat. Then to MOM.)* I'm gonna do right by you, my friend.

MOM: I know.

SPANISH's phone vibrates.

SPANISH: I gotta take this. I'll be back in fifteen.

ANNA: Okay.

He goes.

SPANISH: (*As he leaves.*) Hello, Nurse Hector here. One moment, please.

SPANISH bounds outside.

OUTDOOR, sequence begins, simultaneous to the following HOSPITAL sequence:

	RAE: Hello?
ANNA: I suspect the best way to tell Rae might be to simply hand her the paperwork.	
MOM: Anna.	
	RAE: Huh… hello?
ANNA: She likes knowing there is a "right way" and that things are "in order." If it wasn't for you I'd never believe we were related.	
	RAE: Hello? (*She hangs up, to redial.*)
MOM: You really think the best thing is to give her a stack of papers?	

Silence.

ANNA: It would be easiest.

MOM: For?

ANNA: Me.

RAE: Hello. Hello?

SPANISH arrives outdoors, talking into his phone. He places his ID badge in the door again.

SPANISH: Rae-Anna. Hi.

SPANISH meets RAE, to show her she is on the phone with him.

RAE looks at her phone, befuddled.

SPANISH extends his hand.

SPANISH: I'm Nurse Hector. NP. Your Mom's –

RAE: Holy shit.

SPANISH: Yeah. We've emailed.

ANNA: I don't want to have to speak it.

MOM: Try.

ANNA: Okay.

MOM: No, try it right now.

ANNA: To you?

MOM: Sure.

RAE: Really?

SPANISH: Really.

RAE: This is not a joke Anna is playing on me?

ANNA: Okay. I'll try.

SPANISH holds out his hospital ID to RAE. RAE pulls medical tape from her pocket.

RAE: You put this in the door, before. So I could get back in.

SPANISH: Yeah. I was gonna see if you could talk, but… you were busy.

ANNA: Do I pretend you're her? Or you?

MOM: Ummm. Her. Probably more helpful.

ANNA: Okay. *(Beat.)* Rae.

MOM gets the giggles.

RAE gives SPANISH the medical tape, and then…

RAE: Well, then. *(She pulls out a joint.)* Puff?

SPANISH: I… thank you. I'm at work. So…

MOM: (*Trying to stop laughing.*) Sorry!

RAE: Right.

SPANISH: Otherwise, I'd… I mean there's lots of studies on the merits of CBD.

RAE: Yes! Indeed.

MOM: (*Getting her laughter under control momentarily.*) Okay.

SPANISH: I prefer edibles.

RAE: Hah.

ANNA: I know this might upset you, but I hope you understand it's Mom's choice – She's not gonna be laughing, Mom, help me out!

MOM: Sorry!

MOM tries to quell the giggles.

ANNA: Thank you.

RAE: So you're Nurse Hector. God. If I thought Anna was gonna be pissed off before…

SPANISH: She's pretty resilient. You all are.

ANNA: Rae…

RAE: Yeah. Um. I need a… (*Moment. Time to process.*)

ANNA: This is Mom's choice. This is what she thought would be best for both of us.

MOM: All of us.

ANNA: Huh?

RAE: I'm gonna go for a little walk.

MOM: Well, for you two and Rae's girls.

ANNA: Right. Nice. Okay… this is what she thought would be best for all of us.

SPANISH: Okay. You okay?

RAE: Fine. Thank you.

RAE walks away but doesn't leave. SPANISH deflates, thinking she's gone.

ANNA: It's also why she thought the girls should stay at school. She thought it might be a bit much for them.

MOM: Exactly.

ANNA: Spanish is here because Mom chose him for a very big purpose.

SPANISH: Livin' the dream.

MOM: Too Oprah-sounding.

ANNA: What? It isn't.

SPANISH: Great job, son.

MOM: Ya, try something simpler.

ANNA: Hmmm… um, Mom chose him for a very big… favour.

SPANISH: Regular Lawrence Nightingale.

MOM: *(Laughing.)* "Favour"! Like he's watering my plants while I'm in Vegas.

ANNA: Well, what word is best?

MOM: No, no, "favour" is good. Sorry. Keep going.

RAE turns back to SPANISH, exhaling smoke as she goes. She has a hand outstretched.

RAE: It's nice to meet you.

They shake hands.

SPANISH: Yeah.

ANNA: Spanish is very well respected by his colleagues.

RAE: Are you Native?

ANNA: He's an ideal choice for this… favour.

SPANISH: Yeah.

MOM: You're talking like Rae.

ANNA: I thought it might help.

SPANISH: But I don't know what kind.

RAE: Don't worry about it. You get used to it.

SPANISH: Really?

RAE: No. Come on.

RAE heads to the door and SPANISH follows. They go back inside.

MOM: Talk like you. From your heart. That's why you're the one telling her.

ANNA: Mom!

MOM: Good thing I asked you to practise, geez. Okay, try again. Maybe instead of "very big favour" try "important task."

ANNA: I don't wanna do this anymore. Practise. You'll hear me when I tell her anyway.

MOM: Oh, come on! Spoilsport.

ANNA: I'm not a spoilsport, you're a Russian judge.

MOM: They are always hard on our skaters, aren't they?

ANNA: Yeah.

MOM: Oh, don't pout.

ANNA: I'm not.

MOM: Come on! What's the matter?

ANNA: Well, you're dying, Mom, and there's nobody sticking around who's going to look after me.

MOM: Anna.

ANNA: You know how Rae is. Everything's going to be about her. Even her girls, I bet, will be taking care of her feelings instead of the other way around. It's too much!

MOM: You have Spanish.

ANNA: Yeah. Imagine how great that's gonna go afterwards. Hey, Nurse Hector. Now that you've completed Mom's important task, wanna go to the movies Friday night?

MOM: He'll be all "Ya. A slasher flick!"

ANNA: Very funny.

MOM: A sleeper hit!

ANNA: Ha ha ha.

MOM: Come on, I'm funny.

ANNA: A little.

MOM: Come 'ere.

MOM hugs her for a little while.

You'll get by without me. You hardly needed me since you were four or five.

ANNA: That's not true.

MOM: As soon as I had Rae-Anna, you shifted into little mama mode.

ANNA: You wouldn't let me have a puppy.

MOM: You adored her. You even changed diapers!

ANNA: A whole family of weirdos.

MOM: Remember when you had that doctor's appointment in grade two?

ANNA: Ear infection.

MOM: It was right after Rae's dad passed. I just got out of the hospital and got you girls back.

ANNA: Your arm was still in a sling.

MOM: They'd put us in that little apartment.

ANNA: As if they stuck us on East Hastings. Even way back then.

MOM: I had my two girls on my own for the first time. I knew I had to get everything perfect. That child welfare would be circling like vultures –

ANNA: Total vultures.

MOM: – waiting for me to mess up. I reminded you about that appointment over and over so we'd get it right. I just assumed you knew I'd be coming to take you there.

ANNA: I couldn't hear very well, you know. I had a friggin' ear infection.

MOM: So you get yourself on a bus downtown and arrive on time, all by yourself. Don't even know how they let you on the bus.

ANNA: Well, I didn't pay fare. I just showed the driver my note.

MOM: Imagine, he let a little kid on the bus by herself!

ANNA: Probably figured I was some neglected little Indian.

They laugh.

MOM: As if! You had the neatest braids and the whitest little ankle socks! Anyone could see you were loved.

Beat.

ANNA: I didn't know if you were coming. So I didn't wait to find out.

MOM: I'd been back for over a week.

ANNA: You were back as suddenly as you'd gone. I had no reason to think you'd stay.

MOM: I'd been in the accident, Anna.

ANNA: You said yourself it wasn't an accident. "Not the way he drank."

MOM: I'm sorry, Anna-Rae.

ANNA: I know.

MOM: He seemed like my only choice. That man, his ministry. When I ran from school on my own, plumping up with you, I didn't think I'd ever have my own life. A single mom in the 1950s?

ANNA: And brown as you.

MOM: As you. (*A moment.*) You know, Anna-Rae. I think if I had been as brown as you they wouldn't even have let me try to keep you for myself. They would have taken you when you were born.

ANNA: You're probably right, Mom.

MOM: But we survived. And it was his flock that looked after you girls when I was laid up in hospital.

ANNA: They were horrible.

MOM: I'm so sorry.

ANNA: They kept telling us they didn't know if you'd ever recover. And they didn't let us go see you, so I just had no idea.

MOM: I'm so sorry.

ANNA: The thing about it, Mom, that was so disorienting, is that you were always there before. You were the one thing. No matter where we lived or with who, there was always you. So that one night when you didn't come home, I just… every terrible possibility opened up. And it ate me. My trust.

MOM: I'm sorry, Anna-Rae.

ANNA: Thank you. (*Beat.*) We're here now.

MOM: We're here now.

ANNA snuggles into MOM.

Low, they hum MOM's Travelling Song together.

Towards the end, RAE and SPANISH come in, quietly.

SPANISH: Her drum is here.

A beat as ANNA returns to the room, in her energy.

ANNA: You brought it?

SPANISH: It was on her list. It's in the car with the other things.

RAE: We should have it in here.

ANNA: Uh…

SPANISH: Everything?

RAE: Sure.

SPANISH: I should… get it?

RAE: That would be great. Thank you.

SPANISH goes.

ANNA: What did I miss?

RAE: We met. Outside. I didn't know he was Nurse Hector. From the… care worker list.

ANNA: Okay…

RAE: You were both saying "Spanish." So I didn't know.

ANNA: Right.

RAE: He's Native.

ANNA can't even respond.

MOM laughs.

He seems very devoted to his work.

ANNA: He's… yeah.

RAE: They said we can smudge in the chapel. Oddly.

ANNA looks at her, surprised.

We asked. I knew you'd want to. Eventually.

ANNA: Well. We'll smudge where we please. Thank you.

RAE: It's a hospital. People have… respiratory issues.

ANNA: Well, they don't have to thank us.

RAE: Anna.

ANNA only smiles.

Beat.

ANNA: Rae. Do you remember when the accident happened?

RAE: Not much.

ANNA: Good.

RAE: I was only three. My whole world was you and Mom. I remember she was gone for a while. But you weren't scared, so I wasn't either.

ANNA: I was scared.

Beat.

We shared a tiny bed when we stayed with those people. Your dad's… family? Whoever they were.

RAE: They were mean.

ANNA nods.

ANNA: You asked me if Mom was dying. I told you I'd tell you if she was dying. You made me promise.

RAE only looks at ANNA.

And I promised myself I'd never let Mom get tucked away in a hospital again.

RAE: You were only six.

MOM: Going on twenty. My big girl.

ANNA: Yeah. *(Beat.)* Please understand, Rae; moving her here, to Toronto. It wasn't against you.

RAE: I'm… I'll understand some day. But right now, I'm just…

ANNA: Okay.

RAE: Paining.

ANNA: Okay.

Silence.

What did you and Spanish talk about?

RAE: His work credentials. And the scientific benefits of CBD.

ANNA laughs.

SPANISH returns. He has something wrapped in cloth in his hand and a beautiful, large bag slung over his shoulder.

SPANISH: Laughter. That's a good sign.

RAE: We were talking about you.

SPANISH: Hey…

MOM: *(To herself.)* Hoka hey!

ANNA: What did you two talk about?

SPANISH: The merits of smudging. I mean, on a scientific level. Then we went to the chapel to ask about smudging in the hospital. They said we could. Oddly.

ANNA: Hm.

RAE: It's true.

SPANISH passes ANNA a small cloth wrapped bundle. Within is an abalone smudge shell and some ash.

ANNA: Her prayers.

RAE: I wonder what they were.

MOM: They were for you.

SPANISH: I just wrapped it up, as is. As per her instructions.

ANNA: I should find a place for them.

RAE: There's a big pine right out that way. Can see it from here.

ANNA: Perfect. Anyone wanna come?

SPANISH and RAE speak the following lines simultaneously:

SPANISH: Sure.

RAE: I'll stay here.

ANNA: Okay. Be right back.

RAE: 'Kay.

MOM speaks to RAE but RAE does not know that she can hear MOM. RAE never looks at her.

MOM: You haven't told her.

RAE: Mom. I haven't told her.

Beat. RAE closes her eyes.

God, Mom! I wish I could talk to you.

MOM: You are, my girl.

RAE: I wish you could talk to me.

MOM: My Rae-Anna. So stubborn.

OUTDOORS:

ANNA and SPANISH arrive outside. ANNA goes to the pine tree, SPANISH props the door open with his ID badge.

ANNA takes some tobacco and offers it to the tree. She then sets the ashes at the base of the tree.

RAE: I don't know how to… I wasn't going to text it to her! She never picks up the phone. She shouldn't have gone away!

MOM: And now that you're here together?

RAE walks away and looks out the window where she sees her sister giving the ashes back to the land, SPANISH giving ANNA room.

RAE: I'm the one who had to cross the whole country! Because she moved you here.

MOM: You may as well learn to love everything about her. She's the only sister you got. And she's never going to change.

RAE: She'll never change. And neither will I.

MOM: I know. And I love you for it.

MOM and RAE speak the following lines simultaneously:

MOM: Both my girls are strong minded, self-actualized women and I'm proud as hell.

RAE: *(In a whisper.)* "Both my girls are strong minded, self-actualized women and I'm proud as hell."

ANNA: Was her regalia on that list?

SPANISH: It was.

ANNA: Oh gawd, I can't catch my breath.

SPANISH: Ground yourself.

ANNA sits on the ground and lays her hands flat, feeling Mother Earth.

ANNA: Who will I be when she goes?

SPANISH: You'll be everyone who loves you. Including Battleaxe.

ANNA nods, hearing, absorbing. She takes some good breaths.

ANNA: The sky will brighten soon.

SPANISH: Anna. Do you want me to lay out her regalia?

ANNA: I think it will help me tell Rae.

SPANISH: I'll go do that. Give you time.

ANNA: Thank you, Hector.

She reaches for his hand. He takes hers in both of his. After a moment, she withdraws.

He goes. She prays.

RAE: Why do you have to go?

MOM: I'm tired, my girl. Getting old is tough, but the alternative is tougher. Until it isn't. And then it's time to go.

RAE: Are you scared?

MOM: A little. Mostly I'm scared of how sad you'll be.

RAE: I'm scared. Ugh! Sorry. You shouldn't have to look after me in this.

MOM: It's what I do.

ANNA heads back inside. She finds SPANISH's ID badge on her way in.

RAE: I'm sure you're tired of it. All of it.

MOM: Not of you. Of being in this body. This world. I have so much love for you. And all my loves, but especially my girls. You know that.

RAE: I don't know how to not have you around.

MOM: I'll miss you, too.

RAE: I always feel so proud to be out and about with you. People treat me different when we're together. I won't ever feel that again.

MOM: That's just because I'm an ornery old bag. They're scared of me.

RAE: I'll miss seeing white dudes cower as you send back your soup.

MOM: I was never hard on the skinny little zitty ones. Just their managers.

They laugh, and RAE shifts into crying.

ANNA enters. Puts an arm around her sister.

RAE: I don't even know which thoughts in my head are mine and which are hers.

ANNA: I know.

RAE: Everything I am comes from this woman.

ANNA: Yeh.

RAE: And you.

ANNA is quiet.

MOM: Tell her.

RAE: I hear her voice in my head so clearly. I can have whole conversations with her, all by myself. Is that gonna change?

ANNA: Not if you keep doing it. As often as you do now.

RAE: Aw, you don't know! You've never had your mom die, either.

ANNA: No shit.

RAE: So stop pretending you know!

ANNA: I know what I know, Rae. I'm not apologizing for that.

RAE: "I'm not apologizing for that."

ANNA: Oh, that's super mature.

RAE: "I know what I know, Rae. I'm super mature!"

ANNA: Thank you for the trip back to grade three. Awesome.

RAE: "Awesome. I'm so awesome. My body is smart and my mind is flexible."

MOM: Stop this, girls.

ANNA: Really clever, Rae. I have no idea why you flunked out of university.

MOM: BE KIND TO EACH OTHER!

They all fall silent.

ANNA: I'm sorry.

MOM: You heard me. Now tell her. NOW.

ANNA: I have to tell you something.

RAE: I have to tell YOU something.

ANNA: Oh my god.

RAE: I do though, Anna! I feel like I owe you an apology even though you don't know what I did. Or tried. And failed.

ANNA: Rae, what?

RAE: I tried finding our grandmother. Mom's mom.

ANNA: You did?

RAE: Mom said it was okay.

MOM: I didn't know you tried.

RAE: Hit a dead end. *(Beat.)* Three years of archives and requesting information and being on hold and knocking down doors. I was hoping to come here with a thick file and lots of phone numbers. Names of cousins, aunties… I wanted to give that to you. Us.

ANNA: Where did you even start?

RAE: The school. They have some archives there.

ANNA: Right. And there's a museum in it now.

RAE: And a band office.

ANNA: A daycare too, isn't there?

RAE: Little Fawn Daycare.

MOM: That school.

ANNA: I've never gone in.

RAE: I asked the archivist if there was ever any record of a priest being noted as the father of a child.

ANNA: Not a chance.

RAE: Yeah. She said no. Not that she's seen. But she has lots of relatives who know otherwise.

ANNA: Fuck.

MOM: Girls lived on one side, boys on the other. The clergy went wherever, took whoever they wanted.

RAE: I found Mom's vaccination and baptism records. Under each parent name it said "unknown."

MOM and ANNA speak the following lines simultaneously:

MOM: They knew.

ANNA: They would damn well have known.

MOM: That's why nobody else laid a hand on me.

RAE: The archivist said that's a good clue the mother was still a student and the father was clergy.

MOM: One of those black robes was my blood.

ANNA: Ah, those kids!

MOM: And if he found out who Ronnie was to me, they would have punished him completely.

ANNA: Open prey!

MOM: He would not survive.

RAE: Yes.

MOM drifts in and out from the world of the living to the place of the family she knew as a child – the other students who have already passed.

MOM: Lila! My friend! Is that you?

RAE: I looked for names of every girl who could possibly have been pregnant at that school, nine months before Mom's birthday.

MOM: You're so little.

ANNA: Just little kids.

MOM: We have to help each other out.

RAE: I'm talking about kids who were Keira's age.

MOM: Buddy up. Senior girls with junior girls.

RAE: And younger. Can you imagine?

ANNA: At least Mom had a boy she loved.

MOM: Don't go into the laundry alone.

RAE: Then I looked at which names didn't return the following year.

MOM: Buddy up.

RAE: Grades six through twelve.

ANNA: So young.

MOM: So you don't get taken. But if you do –

ANNA: My god.

MOM: Try to help each other keep it a secret.

ANNA: Those beautiful souls.

MOM: If they figure it out, they'll throw you down the stairs.

RAE: There were so many.

MOM: Starve you in the cellar.

ANNA: Mom.

MOM: Lila. Gone. Violet. Taken.

ANNA: If she hadn't run, she could've…

MOM: Helen. Grace. Where…?

RAE: Then I started trying to find all of those kids.

MOM: So many lost. Taken.

RAE: Or, I mean, their families.

MOM: But us? We can get out. Get away.

RAE: But it's hard to find women who were children in the 1950s.

MOM: Ronnie. (*Time overlapping for her, MOM shouts up at a window.*) Ronnie! Aren't you coming? (*She finds a pebble and throws it.*)

RAE: Last names change.

MOM: Ronnie. Please. We'll get married.

RAE: Deaths went unmarked.

MOM: Ronnie, please. It's me. Your home sweet home.

ANNA: Deaths were covered up.

MOM: Ronnie, where are you?

RAE: And people sometimes don't want to remember. It was like hunting ghosts.

MOM: There's ghosts out here. Ronnie?

ANNA: Mom.

MOM: I have to go.

RAE: I wanted so badly to give us that. All of us. But I couldn't.

MOM: Before they take me.

ANNA: Records were destroyed, Rae. People were hired to destroy tons of records.

MOM: (*In panic.*) Lila? Is that you? Violet?

ANNA: You didn't fail. The world has failed us.

MOM: We thought you were lost.

RAE: I keep thinking of my beautiful girls.

MOM: Helen! Grace?

RAE: Imagine. If we were still forced to send our babies there?

ANNA: If Mom hadn't run from there, we would've…

MOM: So many… run! (*MOM gasps, then falls silent.*)

We hear the absence of her heartbeat.

RAE: Oh my God.

ANNA: Mom!

RAE: Press the call button!

ANNA does, while calling –

ANNA: Spanish!

SPANISH: I'm here!

SPANISH enters. He takes MOM's hand, checks her pulse.

Battleaxe? You still with us?

Heartbeat returns. Only ANNA-RAE consciously hears MOM.

MOM: Ronnie?

SPANISH: Hey.

RAE: Her eyelids!

ANNA: Mom.

SPANISH: Hey, Buddy.

MOM: Cotton puff.

SPANISH: Hey.

ANNA: Mom.

MOM: My girls.

SPANISH: Your girls are here.

MOM: Is it time to cross?

ANNA: Mom.

SPANISH: You're here with us.

RAE: Is she breathing?

SPANISH: She's breathing.

RAE: Jesus Christ!

ANNA: What happened?

SPANISH: Just checking if we're paying attention, I guess.

RAE: Well. We are!

ANNA: Fuck.

MOM: I was looking for Ronnie. He couldn't come.

SPANISH: We're okay.

MOM: I have to go to him.

ANNA: Mom. Breathe gently. We're all here. We'll help you home.

MOM: Time to go.

RAE: She's not going home. She just died! For – ten seconds? Twenty? How long was that?

SPANISH: Not... necessarily. At times there can be twenty or thirty seconds between breaths.

RAE: That's not enough. Can you grab a doctor?

SPANISH: *(After looking at ANNA.)* I can try.

ANNA: Thank you.

RAE: Goddamnit, I should have kept her at your place, Anna. I'm sorry.

ANNA: You panicked, Rae.

RAE: I was being selfish. I wanted to be in charge, and I knew you'd be out of your element here.

ANNA: You're right.

RAE: I know it's been better for her to be here with you, and it tears me up.

ANNA: It doesn't mean she wasn't happy out in Vancouver all those years. Close to you. She just couldn't face being holed up in an institution again.

RAE: I know.

ANNA and RAE hold each other.

I have to say something now.

ANNA: Okay.

RAE draws up her courage and then dives into her phone screen.

What are you – ?

RAE: Just wait. Please. This is from six months ago. Christmas. When Mom was with us. In Vancouver.

RAE plays the video she looked at in the beginning. MOM sounds and looks like her body age.

<u>VIDEO:</u>

MOM: Rae-Anna. Are you taking a picture right now?

RAE: No.

MOM: Oh. Okay. That would be weird.

They laugh a little.

RAE: No kidding!

MOM: So, anyways… I found the guy. He's a licensed nurse practitioner. A man. Who's a nurse!

RAE: Why wouldn't you just get a doctor like a normal person?

MOM: Normal? I've never been accused of that in my life.

RAE: You don't have to tell me.

MOM: I just want to make sure I don't end up plugged in for a hundred years.

RAE: Well. Even plugged in you wouldn't make it that long.

MOM: Have you seen those new light bulbs? Some of them claim to last ten years! Used to be you'd get a couple months out of a light bulb, now it's ten years! Who knows what they'll be able to do for people soon.

RAE: That would be something.

MOM: Hm?

RAE: Government paying to keep an Indian alive.

MOM: Indian woman!

They laugh.

First time for everything.

RAE: First time my mom ever told me she wants me to put her down like a lame horse.

MOM: Honey, it won't be you. You just have to make sure it all happens the way it should.

RAE sighs.

You have to help me get all the paperwork.

RAE: Don't want to.

MOM: Well, your sister isn't able to. You are.

RAE: You think so?

MOM: I know it. You each have your own strengths. I need you both. Both my girls are

MOM and RAE speak the following lines simultaneously:

MOM: strong minded, self-actualized women and I'm proud as hell.

RAE: strong minded, self-actualized women…

RAE: I'm proud too, Mom.

MOM: Good. Now look at this list I made. They're my terms, but we need a lawyer to make it all official. I know that much by now. Gotta get it in black and white while I still have a couple marbles.

RAE: Having to wear diapers is hardly a cause to kill yourself, Mom.

MOM: To each her own.

RAE: But, come on! We all started out that way.

MOM: Sure. But babies hold that wisdom of just having come to earth. They aren't carrying all that knowing from having been here too long.

RAE: You haven't been here too long.

MOM: Not yet. But when I'm on my way out, I want out. I'm sorry, my girl, but that's how I feel. What I know.

Silence between MOM and RAE in the video.

RAE pauses the video.

RAE: (*To ANNA.*) Are you okay?

ANNA: Is there more?

RAE: Yes. I just wanted to make sure you're –

ANNA: I'm okay.

MOM and RAE speak the following lines simultaneously:

MOM: Are you sure?

RAE: Are you sure?

ANNA: I'm okay.

MOM: You're not saying anything.

ANNA: Go ahead, Rae-Anna. If Mom wanted you to tell me, finish telling me.

RAE: Okay.

MOM: You're doing beautifully.

RAE unpauses the video.

VIDEO:

MOM: We had our own ways, back in the day. Now we have to follow the rules here. So you don't end up in the clink.

RAE: *(Small laugh.)* "The clink."

MOM: Plus, I'd probably put up a fight if you tried it any other way. You'd be pressing that pillow onto my face and I'd just be whaling on ya!

RAE: Mom, I will NOT smother you!

MOM: Well, that's why we're getting a professional.

RAE: That's creepy.

MOM: He's not creepy. He's gentle.

RAE: Hm.

MOM: You wanna meet him?

RAE: No!

MOM: You don't have to. Was just askin'.

RAE: How did you find him?

MOM: He –

RAE: No! I don't wanna know. Never mind.

MOM: Okay.

RAE: But I'd like to see his credentials.

MOM: I knew you would. I brought you a copy of his "credentials." They're in my purse.

RAE: How will he do it?

MOM: It's injections. One calms me down and makes sure I won't feel pain. The next one kicks me in the bucket.

They laugh again.

RAE: That's not the expression.

MOM: Well, whatever. It finishes me off.

RAE: You sure you don't wanna move back here?

MOM: I got a cool new place out in Toronto, Rae-Anna. With your big sister. You know that.

RAE: Yeah.

MOM: Me and Anna-Rae take the streetcar for Chinese sometimes. And we go to the Native Centre for women's groups!

RAE: Not surprising.

MOM: We have fun. But you know my home is always where my girls are. Home is when we're all together.

RAE: Okay.

MOM: What are you looking at that pocket phone for, anyways? You got a hot date?

RAE: No, I was recording this.

MOM: What? What for?

RAE: So people don't think I'm making it up.

MOM: Oh, for pete's sake! Nobody would think that.

RAE: Anna would!

MOM: She wouldn't.

RAE: She thinks I'm a bully!

MOM: You can be.

RAE: Mom!

MOM: Well! You're the little sister, but she's the only one who ever had a black eye. And stitches, that one time.

RAE: I just have better aim.

MOM: Well, you can shut that thing off. We're gonna do that official paperwork anyways, so nobody's gonna say boo about it. It's legal now, so bully to them anyways!

RAE: Okay, Mom. I'll call our lawyer today.

MOM: Thank you. You're gonna use up all your tape.

RAE: It's not tape, Mom, it's right on the phone.

MOM: Whatever.

RAE: Remember how I told you about Walkmen and the girls' MP3 players? It's like that, but – oh! I think I found the 'Off' bu – "

The video clicks off.

They are silent. RAE looks at ANNA. ANNA looks at MOM.

ANNA: Well. Kick me in the bucket.

They laugh.

RAE: No!

ANNA: Ah, Rae-Anna.

RAE: Oh, Anna-Rae.

ANNA: What am I gonna do with you?

RAE: Same as I do with you.

They hug.

Are you upset?

ANNA: A little.

RAE: I think she had to tell me because of the girls. I mean, I have to look after them in this, too. So she wanted me to have lots of warning. To help with that.

ANNA: Yeah.

RAE: Are you mad she told me? Instead of you?

ANNA: No.

Silence.

RAE: I don't think she woulda been crazy about how I told you, but…

ANNA: It was perfect. You did great.

RAE: Really?

ANNA: Truly. You did good by me. Us.

RAE: Thank you, Anna. I'm sorry I couldn't find her mom. Our grandma.

ANNA: Me, too. But your girls know their grandma. Our mom. That's a big deal.

RAE: Yes. It is. I been realizing… ever since Mom told me about this whole assisted death thing. When she gave me that responsibility, to tell you? I realized I'm created from love, too. Love of you two. And that brought me to my own girls. And your love with them. And even my husband who you hate. All of that makes me who I am.

ANNA: I don't hate him.

RAE: You don't like him.

ANNA: No.

RAE: You asshole.

Laughter.

There's one other thing.

ANNA: I don't know how much more I can handle.

RAE: It's about Spanish. Don't be angry with him. Or me. I chose not to know him ahead of time, so I didn't know.

ANNA: Okay.

RAE: The doctor. Or – nurse. Doing the procedure… ceremony… for Mom. It's Spanish. Only I knew him as Nurse Hector, so I didn't know it was him.

ANNA: You two talked about this outside.

RAE: I asked him to let me tell you. That Mom asked me to take care of things this way.

ANNA: I see.

SPANISH comes in. He's holding a box of doughnuts.

(Bursts out laughing.) Why do you have doughnuts?

SPANISH: Rae was saying she'd like a doughnut. But I dunno which kind, so I… I dunno.

RAE laughs with her sister.

RAE: You're really not mad?

ANNA: I'm not mad.

RAE: Not even at him?

ANNA: Not even him. I trust he did everything he could to go about this in the right way. As did the old battleaxe.

ANNA approaches her MOM.

Smarty-pants.

RAE: Is she ever. Geez, I didn't think it would go this well.

MOM: I did.

SPANISH: Everything is… out in the open?

ANNA: Yes. Rae told me everything. Mom asked that it be this way.

SPANISH: Yeah.

ANNA: And you knew the whole time.

RAE: But you're not mad at him.

SPANISH: The doc on call can't come. She's with another patient. And your Mom has a DNR, so…

RAE: Got it.

ANNA hugs SPANISH.

SPANISH: I'm sorry I haven't set out her regalia yet. I was called to ER to help with a transfer.

ANNA: Strong drum.

MOM: It's time.

RAE: I think it's time. Is it time?

ANNA: I think so.

SPANISH: We can ready her as she wished. And then I'll review the steps of the procedure. And we'll… do as she asked.

RAE: I brought an, um…

ANNA helps RAE pull a large bundle from under somewhere. They unwrap it.

Even though we still don't know where our grandma is from. At least we know where we're from, right? Where Mom was born. And who we call home.

ANNA: And who we call home.

RAE and ANNA reveal a button blanket.

Rae.

RAE: Rae-Anna.

ANNA: My Rae-Anna.

RAE: My Anna-Rae.

MOM is softly humming her Travelling Song, growing calmer, peaceful.

RAE and ANNA spread out the blanket. We see its full sun design.

ANNA: Wow.

MOM: The sun!

RAE: Yeah.

ANNA looks to SPANISH, who picks up the beautiful bag he brought in and helps the women with the items.

First, a long ribbon skirt from her Anishnaabe friends.

ANNA: The memorial I mentioned? That woman – Rose. She made this for Mom.

RAE: There's some mauve in it.

ANNA and RAE laugh lightly.

SPANISH passes ANNA some small adornments for MOM's hair.

ANNA: These are some hair ties from her friend Monique in Six Nations.

RAE: And where did she get her drum?

ANNA: She made it.

RAE: Seriously?

ANNA: Ya! There was a drum-making workshop in a park. She went all by herself and, of course, made a bunch of friends. Margo, the woman who led it, taught her how to feast it and care for it.

RAE: Feels like things I should have known.

ANNA: There's still time.

RAE: I mean… about her.

ANNA hands RAE the drum. RAE opens a palm and circles the face of the drum gently.

Was it this Margo who taught her the song?

ANNA: Probably. Which one?

RAE: The girls said there's a song. That you're supposed to sing for Mom. When it's time.

ANNA: Yeah.

RAE: You taught it to them. Ceilidh and Keira.

ANNA: Yes. Actually her friend Faith gave her that song. So she can share it with anyone she wants. She wanted it to be sung in your home, too.

RAE: They sang it on here for me. So I could learn it. To sing with you. If it's okay.

ANNA: Absolutely.

RAE: Okay. Oh, but I… even though I… *(She does the joint smoking gesture again, and hands the drum back to ANNA.)*

SPANISH: For some people, it's been a medicine for always. Right?

ANNA: *(Skeptical, but giving.)* True.

Beat. ANNA sets the drum in the place she feels it should be, with MOM.

Should we let the girls bring us in?

RAE: Hm?

ANNA: Play it. What they taped for you. And we'll join in.

SPANISH: I can come back –

RAE: No. Mom wants you here.

ANNA confirms with a nod.

RAE starts playing the recording.

As the song moves, RAE becomes stronger in her voice.

SPANISH hands ANNA the moccasins she found for MOM.

Each sister puts a gorgeous Lakota Sioux moccasin on MOM's feet.

ANNA checks MOM, who seems so very still.

ANNA: Mom?

SPANISH takes MOM's wrist in his hand and waits for a pulse. He sets her arms down and he nods his head. Yes, she's gone.

The two sisters hold each other.

The singing on the recording – the young women's voices – continues. An impossible number of voices ebb and flow through time and space with them. All of the grandmothers, from all times.

MOM slowly rises from the bed, singing the final round with her granddaughters. They don't see her go, but they feel her begin to travel home.

End of play.

Honour Beat Study Guide

The original play guide for *Honour Beat* was created by Theatre Calgary for the premiere production in 2018. The principal author of the guide was Jamie Tymchuk, and the essay "The Severed Bond and the Awakening Spirit" was written by Steve Gin. Our thanks to the authors and to Theatre Calgary for permission to reprint excerpts from the guide in this edition of the play.

Interesting Facts

- The Canadian Constitution recognizes three groups of Indigenous persons: First Nations, Inuit, and Métis. These are three distinct peoples with unique languages, histories, cultural and spiritual beliefs. Indigenous persons continue to advocate for the right to self-identify.
- More than 1.67 million Canadians identify as Indigenous.
- The last residential school operated by the Canadian government closed in 1996 in Saskatchewan. At its peak in the early 1930s, it is estimated there were approximately 80 schools with more than 17,000 enrolled students.
- Medical Assistance in Dying, or MAID, is recently-passed Canadian government legislation. Participants must meet the eligible criteria, and the service must be overseen by a physician or licensed nurse practitioner.

Terms to Know

- *Sundance:* A sacred ceremony performed by some Indigenous people in honour of the sun. It usually involves a community gathering and praying for healing. Individuals may make personal sacrifices, such as fasting.

- *Matriarch:* A strong woman who is head of a family or tribe.
- *Moccasins:* Historically the footwear of Indigenous people of North America. Often made of deerskin or other soft leather.
- *Smudging:* A ceremony practised by some Indigenous people, that involves the burning of sacred herbs, in some cases for spiritual cleansing or blessing. (More information about smudging can be found in the following pages.)
- *Elder:* Indigenous Elders can be men, women, or non-binary persons with deep spirituality that has earned them respect among their community. An Elder's duties might include conducting smudging ceremonies or leading an opening prayer.
- *Fasting:* A willing abstinence from food and/or drink for a period of time, as part of ceremony.
- *Medicine Wheel:* A circle that represents the alignment and connection of oneself to the natural and spiritual world, through physical, emotional, mental, and spiritual realities. It can be displayed in various ways and the significance and use can differ among Indigenous cultures.

The Art of Smudging

Spiritual smoke created from the burning of sacred and/or medicinal plants and herbs is practised in many cultures and religions around the world. In Canada, it is a common practice with many Indigenous peoples and is referred to as "smudging."

Since there are many Indigenous groups and this is a traditional practice, there are various beliefs and ceremonies regarding smudging that are unique to each specific culture. However, most smudging traditions share certain elements. For instance, although anyone can smudge, smudging ceremonies are often led by an Elder or spiritual leader. Smudging is often done in times of needed healing or prayer. All smudging ceremonies require a shell, fireproof bowl, smudge stick, rock, or ball in which the plants and herbs are lit. The smoke created is believed to have healing and cleansing properties that a person inhales as it is wafted over the face and body, either with their hand(s), a fan, or a feather. When a room is being smudged, the smoke is directed around the area and the person conducting the ceremony prays for negative energy to leave and positive energy to remain.

The healing powers of plants is not a new concept. In smudging there are four particular sacred medicinal plants that are often used, and although there are many others, Indigenous peoples usually will utilize these four:

Sacred Tobacco: Tobacco is said to be the pathway to the spirit world, and is often used as an offering or gift. In many Native cultures, tobacco is associated with life events such as birthing rituals, courtship, marriage, death, and prayer. Sacred tobacco may be composed of a blend of plants, such as *kinnikinnick* and the bark of the red osier dogwood.

Sweetgrass: Known for its sweet scent that is intensified when burned, sweetgrass is often used in healing and talking circles. It is believed to purify the spirit, and to eliminate negative thoughts.

Sage: A medicinal plant with strong physical healing properties, white sage is commonly used to release troubles of the mind and / or remove negative energies. White sage smoke is also believed to provide a barrier that prevents negative spirits from entering the room in which the ceremony is being held. Desert sage has properties that protect cells from toxins and organisms in the environment that cause infections; it is anti-fungal, antiseptic, and an astringent.

Cedar: Burned to carry prayers to the Creator, cedar also aids in ridding the mind and body of negative energies and ushering in positive ones. When cedar is burned with tobacco, a crackling occurs, which is said to call the attention of the spirits to the offering that is being made.

Indigenous spiritual traditions such as smudging were greatly repressed during colonization. Although the Indian Act did not explicitly ban smudging, as it did the Sundance (until 1951), it did outlaw Indigenous culture in a broad sense, in which smudging plays a great part. Fortunately, smudging is still prominent today due to Indigenous resistance, and, through the Truth and Reconciliation Commission Calls to Action, we have started to see awareness and acceptance of Indigenous healing practices in Canada. In fact, because Indigenous patients find smudging a vital component of healing and prayer, hospitals are increasingly modifying their policies to accommodate this practice, as shown in *Honour Beat*.

Smudging is an Indigenous tradition that involves deeply spiritual practice, though its use by non-Indigenous peoples continues to increase in popularity. In some cases this can lead to the sale of inauthentic tools and ceremonies that are spiritually and culturally insensitive. If you are interested in smudging ceremonies, it is recommended you respectfully seek advice from those with Indigenous ancestry and ceremonial knowledge. If you are invited to participate in a smudge and are unsure of proper etiquette, ask someone knowledgeable what to do.

Conversation Starters for Further Discussion

- Why do you think the play was called *Honour Beat?* What is the significance of that title?
- Do you relate more to one of the sisters? Why?
- Did your opinion of the sisters change by the end of the play? Why or why not?
- Anna-Rae and Rae-Anna each has a nickname that their mother uses to tease them. Do you have a nickname? How has it affected your identity?
- Families take many shapes. The "nuclear family" is not as common as it was two generations ago. What examples of non-nuclear families can you think of?

The Severed Bond and the Awakened Spirit

by Steve Gin

Though Tara Beagan's play *Honour Beat* does not focus on residential schools, her characters have been deeply affected by them. While they have been affected by the breakdown of family and culture brought on by the schools, these women also draw from the strength and resiliency of Indigenous culture to overcome tremendous odds.

"When the school is on the reserve, the child lives with its parents, who are savages; he is surrounded by savages, and though he may learn to read and write, his habits and training and mode of thought are Indian. He is simply a savage who can read and write."
–Sir John A. Macdonald
Former Prime Minister of Canada, 1883

The notion of these words coming from an elected official in Canada seems shocking but history has clearly recorded these words and their consequences. Though the last of the Canadian residential schools closed in 1996 near Punnichy, Saskatchewan, their effect continues to be felt, even by descendants who have never attended a residential school.

The intention of residential schools has been clear from their beginning: isolation and assimilation of Indigenous peoples, by severing bonds with family, language, and land.

Day schools, run by a combination of Catholic, Anglican, Presbyterian, and Methodist churches, began appearing near Native communities in the 1840s. Drawing from the model of the Carlisle Indian School in the United States, the Canadian government commissioned the 1879 Davin Report, which called for cooperation with churches to implement a network of schools that would pursue an aggressively assimilationist approach. In a letter to Public Works Minister Hector-Louis Langevin, Bishop Vital-Justin Grandin recommended schools be structured so that students "lead a life different from their parents and cause them to forget the customs, habits and language of their ancestors."

In 1883, the first of approximately 139 Canadian residential schools opened near Battleford, Saskatchewan. A year later, an amendment to the Indian Act ordered the compulsory attendance, and removal from their families, of Native children aged seven to sixteen years old. The attack on Indigenous culture was brutal and unforgiving. Speaking one's language was strictly forbidden, with beatings, humiliation, and withholding of food being common punishments. Some students recall their tongues being pierced with pins and nails. Schools confiscated objects that held cultural meaning, such as clothing, traditional objects, and family belongings. Students' long hair and braids were cut off, and children were stripped of their birth names, receiving European ones instead. Amongst residential school survivors, one out of five have reported being sexually abused.

Whether the consistent underfunding of residential schools was deliberate or a breakdown in government policy remains unclear, but the results were consistent: malnutrition, overcrowding, and rampant disease among children who often lacked immunity. Tuberculosis and trachoma were common in these schools. Across Canada, mortality rate varied, and at one point reached a shocking 50% in Alberta.

Not every residential school survivor suffered this magnitude of abuse. A fortunate few, such as celebrated Dene/Suline/Saulteaux painter Alex Janvier, found support and encouragement for his talents from teachers, which played an important role in his professional career. His experience was not without struggle, however, as Janvier lost siblings to tuberculosis in the Blue Quills residential school and suffered intense loneliness. For years he signed his paintings with the number "287" – a stark reminder of the number assigned to him at Blue Quills after being taken from his family. In fact, Indigenous artists have delivered some of the most haunting indictments of the school system, such as a number of recent projects on Chanie Wenjack, detailing the story of a twelve-year-old Anishinaabe boy who escaped his school in 1966, and died of exposure along the railway tracks while trying to return home. Evidence had been mounting for decades about the abuses, but Chanie Wenjack's death sparked a public inquest, hastening the end of the agreement between churches and the federal government to occur three year later. In 1996, the Royal Commission on Aboriginal Peoples recommended a report looking into the long-term effects of the schools, with the long-awaited Truth and Reconciliation Commission of Canada (TRC) being authorized in 2008 to document the stories of survivors and their descendants.

The TRC delivered its report in June 2015 after extensive and sometimes controversial hearings held across Canada, with 94 specific calls to action surrounding Aboriginal child welfare, education, language, culture, health, and justice. History can be a shocking reminder of past abuses, but contemporary Indigenous arts in Canada – be they literary, performing, or visual – signal an awakening of the spirit.